BRIDGE THE GAP & SCORE MORE

DR SHIVANI GOEL

GARIYASI GARG

Made with ❤ on the Notion Press Platform
www.notionpress.com

This book is dedicated to our loving teachers and students.

Contents

Foreword

How we feel in the places where we spend much of the early years of our life shapes our sense of who we are. For a long time, I loved studying and felt at home in the classroom. But recently I began to understand how hard school or college can feel when you're struggling to keep up, and every day feels like you're slipping further behind. My own challenges began when I moved from CBSE to the IB (one of the world's toughest boards) and then to Oxford, where I juggled challenging courses and an online master's degree at the same time. During those years, I picked up countless techniques for revision, motivation, and focus, drawn from books, videos, and experimentation. Each time a new technique stuck and I followed my plans, I rebuilt my confidence and regained my belief that I could reach my ambitions.

Prof. Shivani Goel has spent decades guiding students who once felt lost or left behind. I have seen her help students find their feet, sometimes to the point of not just passing their exams when they were previously failing, but thriving both inside and outside the classroom. One of her students went on become the Valedictorian at her university as well as publishing her own poetry book. This is just one of many examples. She has decided to put all her accumulated wisdom into a book for wider reach.

I, her daughter, am mostly just happy and honored to help.

The biggest flaw in our education system is that it often teaches only to the toppers, letting so much talent just below the surface go unnoticed and unsupported. This book is mainly for you: for any student – young or old –

who has ever felt left behind, unmotivated, or uncertain. We hope it offers you motivation, practical ways to focus, and a sense of happiness in your journey no matter where you start or stand today.

If anything in these pages helps you, let us know through your feedback. If something doesn't resonate, tell us that too; we're always learning, and we want to improve. Not every piece of advice will work for everyone, and that's okay. As the authors of *Make Time* say, "Take what helps, leave the rest."

With hope,

Gariyasi

Preface

This book suggests very simple ways to make a good start on learning something new at any age of life. The content of this self-help book, if followed, aims to make the reader a successful and a learned person capable of achieving their targets.

Students who are struggling with the challenges of attending classes regularly, understanding their subjects and performing well in exams fail to goto a counsellor or mentor for some guidance. Even when they are advised personally by the mentor, the sessions may not be sufficient to bring good results. The purpose of this book is to help such students read these concepts as many times as they want.

Different chapters of the book represent different viewpoints towards being motivated for studies, focusing for better results and increasing productivity. Many methods for balancing your energy are also presented in this book. Each one of the concepts presented here has been taken from personal experience; many students have implemented these successfully and benefitted from this advice.

The book is presented as a conversation between a mentor and a student. At the end of each chapter, few tips are suggested as key takeways that the reader can refer to repeatedly. In addition, each chapter ends with a 'quick adventure.' These are quick and easy tasks that the reader can do to implement the learnt concepts immediately. We highly recommend you go on these quick adventures: taking the first step is like being halfway there!

There are three sections in the book: Motivate Yourself, Focus Techniques and Beyond the Classroom.

Motivate Yourself section has six chapters aimed at motivating the reader for studying.

In the chapter "**Unknown is Scary, Known is Friend**", we discuss that things are scary until we try it! The reader is motivated to start gradually getting familiar with scary subjects.

The chapter "**Breakfast, Lunch, Dinner**" is trying to correlate food timings in a day with timings for various activities. As we eat food at scheduled times for maintaining a good health, we need to study or other activities at their scheduled time to keep a good routine. As skipping meals and eating two meals together can cause harm, skipping classes and reading much content at the same time results in poor results.

The chapter "**Duty-Right Cycle**" aims to motivate the reader to do his/her duty as a student, and honour the privileges or services which he/she is receiving.

When students don't study much and are fearful of failure in exams, they use unfair means like cheating. The chapter "**Sports Spirit**" is trying to correlate the bad consequences of cheating in sports with that of exams, motivating the reader to be a true sportsman and play fair in exams.

The chapter "**Re-taking Exams or Not**" is encouraging the reader to clear their exams in the first attempt. The problems related to appearing for a re-exam (supplementary exam) are presented, and the example of a nutritious diet and taking nutrient supplements is used to explain this.

Sometimes, students lack enthusiasm to study due to problematic relationships, fear of failure, low self- esteem, lack of love and support and many more issues in life. As a result, students have little energy left for studying. The chapter "**Apply Affirmations**" helps the student overcome these issues by saying affirmations for boosting confidence and motivating oneself.

In case the reader is already motivated enough to study, but is not able to perform as per his/her plans or expectations to get good results, one can read the chapters in section 2. In section 2, **FocusTechniques**, various techniques that can help readers in organizing their work and scheduling activities in an efficient way are presented.

The chapter "**Eat Your Pizza Fresh!**" emphasizes that the best way to learn is to concentrate in the class, and to treat studying like eating pizza hot and fresh to enjoy its taste.

The importance of learning in small chunks, slowly but regularly, everyday is presented in chapter "**Learning Alphabets Regularly**", with analogy to learning alphabets in kindergarten.

The chapter "**Series versus Movies**" is an interesting chapter that relates watching series or movies in the theatre or on TV to the approach for studying any subject. If the topics in a subject are in a sequence like a series, one should follow the series method. If there are topics which are independent of the other content of the subject, these can be studied independently like a movie.

One technique for planning your daily activities and monitoring your performance as a way to priorotize is presented in the chapter "**Progress Tracker**".

The chapter "**Pareto Principle (80/20 rule)**" is inspired from Pareto principle or 80/20 rule which says that 20% of causes are responsible for 80% of outcomes, suggesting the reader to focus on the easiest parts of the subject first.

The chapter "**Old Question Papers**" provides useful tips for exam preparation by solving old question papers.

Section 3: "**Beyond the Classroom**" is about the importance of good health, entertainment, good connections and social service.

The chapter "**Healthy is Wealthy**" enforces the reader to follow a health regime and stay healthy. If you're unhealthy, it's going to be very difficult to perform well.

The chapter "**Entertainment as a Reward**" suggests the reader to entertain themselves only at the right times, i.e. after completing the due tasks and not to over-indulge. It also stresses the importance of making time for hobbies, and celebrating one's successes.

The chapter "**Stay Connected**" outlines the benefits of connecting with family members, mentors and friends.

The chapter "**The Power of Helping**" encourages the reader to take part in social service and build their own self-esteem through acts of kindness.

Early in our career, when we started helping others (through teaching at an underprivileged school and tutoring college students), we felt great. This feeling only increased as we put ourselves out to mentor more people. So, we decided to write the last chapter on the power of helping, and this book.

Acknowledgements

We are thankful to our parents, family members and friends for their unconditional love and support.

We also express our gratitude for all our teachers who given us the courage and skills to take up any challenge in life. We thank our colleagues for providing an accommodating work environment. Most importantly, we are grateful to our mentees for believing in us.

Specifically, we are thankful to Prof Deepak Garg for suggesting improvements to the content and the title. We are also grateful to Er. Vishal Goel for making suggestions such as adding 'Key Takeaways' at the end of every chapter. His suggestion to add 'good sleep' as a healthy habit has also been incorporated into the book. We are thankful to Prakriti Garg for her suggestions related to the book cover.

We are thankful to Ms. Usha, Ms. Shikha and Ms. Ashu for their encouragement in writing this book. We hope all students, and Arnav, Ishaan, Ayushi and Avni, will also benefit from it.

Prologue

Happy Reading, and **Implementing**!

Introduction

Student: Hi Ma'am, nice to meet you.

Mentor: Hi! I'm very happy you came. Tell me, how can I help?

Student: I'm really struggling with my studies and personal life. It feels like everyone else is moving forward, but I'm stuck. Sometimes I regret not getting into a better college. Other times, my personal problems affect my studies, and I keep failing and retaking exams. My confidence is low, and I feel very lonely. I don't like anything about my studies anymore and I don't know what to do.

Mentor: Thank you for sharing this. It takes courage to admit when things aren't going well and to ask for help, so you've already taken an important step. I've worked with many students facing similar challenges, and trust me, you're not alone. You can overcome these problems. You can bridge the gap, improve your situation, and feel proud of yourself again.

Student: Really? I'm not sure, but I'm ready to try. What should I do?

Mentor: Bridging the gap involves three important steps. First, it seems you're struggling with motivation—you mentioned feeling hopeless and down. We will use some metaphors to help boost your motivation, especially during tough times. Second, once you're motivated, you need sharp focus. By removing distractions and using simple techniques, you can greatly improve your productivity. Third, remember that your studies and personal life are connected. Learning to balance them, just like planets smoothly orbiting in the solar system, is essential. We'll work together on achieving this balance. For different students, different things prove useful. Some mainly need motivation, others benefit the most from balance, while others find focus game-changing, so feel free to prioritise what feels most important to you as we go. How does this sound?

Student: That sounds great, Ma'am. I'm excited to start. Hopefully, I'll struggle less by the time I finish my degree.

Mentor: I promise you will. Now, can you quickly repeat the key things we'll work on during our mentorship?

Student: Sure!

1. Motivation.
2. Focus techniques.
3. Balancing studies, extra-curriculars and personal life.

Mentor: Fantastic, and don't forget the most important one: never be afraid of asking for help.

Student: Oh yeah, thank you, ma'am!

MOTIVATE YOURSELF

In this section, we discuss various metaphors that can help you get excited about learning again and approach your studies with a positive mindset.

CHAPTER ONE

Unknown is Scary, Known is Friend

Learn by entering the pool and take one step at a time.

Mentor: Oh no, I just saw a lizard and got scared! Do you fear any subject?

Student: Yes, Ma'am! I hate Mathematics. I wish it wasn't in the syllabus. I even have nightmares about it.

Mentor: Many students feel this way about tough subjects. But remember, these subjects won't last forever. You just need to pass them now. Once you clear them, you'll never have to worry about them again!

Student: But when I fear a subject, I avoid studying it, and that makes things worse. How can I handle this?

Mentor: That makes a lot of sense. When we find something scary, we avoid it. Avoiding it makes it stay unknown, and unknown things feel even scarier. It becomes a cycle of fear. The solution is to get to know the subject better.

Once you start to open the door and take a small little step towards knowing this subject, you'll find you can get through it. Let me explain. Do you know how to swim?

Student: Yes, Ma'am. I swim very well and enjoy being in the water.

Mentor: Great! Do you know anyone who is afraid of swimming?

Student: Yes, my sister fears water.

Mentor: How do you encourage her?

Student: I tell her not to worry; there's nothing to fear. She shouldn't just watch from outside and fear drowning. She should slowly enter the water. The more she explores, the sooner she'll learn swimming. It's not difficult. She can use swimming aids in the beginning, and once she gains confidence, she can swim without them.

Mentor: Excellent! You've given the perfect solution for fear of studying to every student. Many students feel studying is difficult and scary. Just like getting into the pool, the solution is simple. When you begin working on a subject you find difficult, it will gradually become easier.

Just like swimming aids, students can also use support methods like revision classes or studying with friends. You can also write to your teacher or mentor and clear your doubts with them to get started. Eventually, you'll become confident enough to study on your own.

Student: That's helpful! Can you tell me more ways of doing this?

Mentor: Sure! Well, you find the subject scary because it is difficult. So, you need to make it easier. To do this,

- Start with the easier portions. Aim to cover 50-60% of the subject that feels manageable first. This will boost your confidence and give you a solid foundation to pass the exam.
- Join a study group and discuss problems with classmates.
- Solve previous years' question papers. This can reduce exam anxiety and give you a sense of familiarity with the pattern of questions.
- Watch easy-to-understand video lessons for beginners. If possible, try to understand the same sub-topic from two or three different short videos. That can help in understanding subjects better, especially difficult ones.

Student: Thank you for these helpful tips, Ma'am. I'll use these to get familiar with new, scary subjects.

Mentor: Remember, you won't have this difficult subject forever. The sooner you face it, the sooner you can move past it!

Student: That makes sense. Usually, I prefer easier subjects and wait for friends to help with the difficult ones. Is it so bad to keep doing that?

Mentor: I appreciate your honesty. It's normal to like easier subjects more – our mind likes these subjects and we need less effort to understand them.

But try to balance your studies. If you focus on a few topics a day, you can mix the subjects you enjoy with at least one touch subject each day.

Student: I'll try to do that, Ma'am. I'll try to not just study my favourite subjects, and spend time on difficult ones too.

Key Takeaways:

- If a subject seems scary, don't avoid it. Take small steps to make it less scary. Familiar = no longer scary.
- Just like swimming aids, use revision aids at first for difficult topics.

Quick Adventure:

Think about which subject is the scariest for you. Now, message or email a senior student or your teacher to ask tips for studying that subject. Ask which parts of the syllabus are the easiest, so you can start with those topics first.

CHAPTER TWO

BREAKFAST, LUNCH, DINNER

Study regularly, and at the right time.

Mentor: Hi! It's great to see you, I just finished my breakfast. How many meals do you have in one day? What happens when you miss a meal at some time of the day?

Student: In one day, we have breakfast, lunch and dinner at set time intervals. If we miss a meal, we may not be able to eat later. For example, if we miss breakfast, next time we eat, it may become lunch because it's the time for lunch and already past time for breakfast. If we try to eat two meals together, our stomach gets upset.

Mentor: Right. So, you have only breakfast at the time of breakfast and lunch at the time of lunch. Similar is the case with studies. There's a right time for meals, and there's also a right time for studies. If you skip one class, you may not have time for re-scheduling it because there will be other classes and work to do later. Just like you cannot eat the entire weeks' food on one day, you cannot do all the studying of the semester in just the last few days.

Student: I see the metaphor now. So, what does study at the right time look like?

Mentor: The best way to stay on track is to regularize studying habits, like reviewing what you have learnt on the same day, rather than cramming everything in one day. This is also key to avoiding stress. This has several benefits:

- You'll have less content to go over daily, making it easier to understand and retain.
- If you have any doubts, you can ask immediately in the next class.
- If current content is the basis for upcoming content, you will be able to understand future content better.

If, by chance, you miss the basics, you may not understand the content shared in the next few or many more classes too. It could hamper your performance in assignments related to that topic's content, leading to confusion, disinterest or even frustration for the subject. Thus, regularity is key. Even if daily study is not possible, at least covering each week's content on the weekend is a good strategy.

Student: This example is helpful Ma'am! I will take care of it.

Key Takeaways:

- Just like we eat meals at regular times to remain healthy, studying regularly helps us prevent last minute stress.

- Just like it's best to eat breakfast in the morning, attending a class and studying for it when it is scheduled is usually the best decision.

Quick Adventure:

Close your eyes for one minute. Imagine how confident and relaxed you'll feel at exam time if you revise regularly—just as you feel energized and healthy after eating meals on time.

CHAPTER THREE

DUTY-RIGHT CYCLE

Fulfil your role with thankfulness and love for your family.

Mentor: Hi dear, what do you expect, and hope for, from your college or hostel when you take admission?

Student: I expect and hope for the best possible environment—clean classrooms, good furniture, a canteen with healthy food, and good facilities like sports and medical care. Since we pay fees, I feel these things are my right.

Mentor: That makes sense. It's important to have a good environment. By the way, are these fees usually paid by you, or your parents?

Student: My parents pay. I love my parents a lot, and I'm grateful they are doing so much for me. Sometimes, parents even take loans just so their children can have a better education.

Mentor: That's right. So, while it's your right to expect a good college, your parents are making big sacrifices for you. What do you feel is your duty to them?

Student: I feel my duty is to take care of myself, stay healthy, make good friends, and do my best in studies. I want to make my parents proud and show them their efforts are worth it.

Mentor: Beautifully said. Everyone has duties—parents, teachers, students. Imagine if the canteen chef decided not to cook properly for a week. How would you feel?

Student: I wouldn't like it at all! It would make life hard, and I'd worry about my health. I would also be stressed because I would need to arrange alternative food for me.

Mentor: Exactly. We all depend on each other. Just as we hope others do their part, we should do ours too. When you skip classes or don't give your best, it doesn't just affect your results—it affects your family too. Instead, if you get high attendance marks, learn new concepts, complete your assignments, and score well in exams, you'll feel great for having done your role as a student well. And, when you remember your love and gratitude for your parents, doing your duty feels natural.

Student: I see what you mean, Ma'am. It's not just about rules but about caring for the people who care for me.

Mentor: Exactly! Remember, your efforts now are a way to thank your parents and take care of yourself too.

Key Takeaways:

- Take care of your health and the company you keep
- Use your time and money wisely

- Remember how grateful you are for your parents' love and support, and use that as motivation to study well.

Quick Adventure:

Call your parents. Tell them you're determined to do well this year and that you're grateful for their support.

CHAPTER FOUR

Sports Spirit

Bounce back and play fair.

Mentor: Hi dear, do you play any sports?

Student: I do! I love playing football.

Mentor: How does a sportsperson aim to win?

Student: Before the game: practice, practice, practice. During the game, a sportsperson aims for 100% concentration in the game. If you lose focus even for a second, you can miss a goal.

Mentor: Correct! And what should you do if you make a mistake during the game, but the game is still going? Should you start feeling sorry, blaming yourself or others?

Student: No, Ma'am! You have to move on from the lost goal right away, recover quickly, and play even harder to make up for it.

Mentor: Exactly! There's no time to dwell on mistakes — you restart with more focus and energy. It's the same with studies. If you get fewer marks in a test, don't waste time feeling bad. Focus fully on the next one. See what you need to study, revise what you know, and work on tough topics in groups with your friends — like how you practise before a match. More practice leads to better results, in both sports and studies. The sports spirit you show in football can help you in your studies too.

Student: Yes, Ma'am! I'll make a timetable for regular revision.

Mentor: Good. Now, what happens if someone breaks the rules in sports or if someone engages in foul play?

Student: The player is disqualified, Ma'am. There are no shortcuts to success.

Mentor: Exactly. Foul play isn't allowed in studies either. Never think of cheating in exams. If you're caught, you lose not only your marks but also face disciplinary action. Cheating can cost you much more than scoring less. If you're not well-prepared, accept your score and prepare better next time. In studies, like in sports, honesty is key.

Student: Yes Ma'am! Honesty is the best policy, everywhere.

Key Takeaways:

- Like a sportsperson on the field, don't dwell too long on mistakes
- Move forward, plan your next step and keep your eyes on the goal
- Honesty is the best policy -- don't cheat in exams

Quick Adventure:

List the qualities of your favourite sports player. Circle one quality you will try to bring into your own studies and work.

CHAPTER FIVE

RE-TAKE EXAMS OR NOT?

Clear it the first time.

Mentor: Hi dear! Could you tell me what a balanced plate of food means to you?

Student: Yes, ma'am. It's a plate that has many kinds of food—spicy, sweet, salty, tangy—so we get all the nutrients we need.

Mentor: Exactly. Your curriculum is like that plate. Some subjects have more theory. Some are practical. A few needs strong memory, others let you be creative. Together, they give you a complete education. Do you think you always have a balanced meal and get all the vitamins you need?

Student: I really don't like green vegetables. The doctor told me to take iron tablets because I don't get enough iron from my diet.

Mentor: Right. These tablets are supplements—extra help for what your regular meals could have given you daily. Which is better? To take supplements or to include iron in your meals?

Student: It's better to include iron in daily meals, I think.

Mentor: Correct. Nutrients from whole foods are better absorbed by the body than supplements. Eating a good diet keeps your body strong and balanced. It's smarter to stay healthy and prevent problems than to grow weak, visit the doctor and fix them later. Like the saying goes: "Prevention is better than cure."

College works the same way. If you cannot move ahead in your course without passing a mandatory subject, it is not wise to ignore it when it is being taught. It's better to study when the subject is taught than to fail and prepare for the re-exam often called supplementary exam, later. How do you feel when you fail a subject and need a supplementary exam?

Student: I feel very bad and disappointed, especially when I fail by one or two marks. But if I didn't study much, I am mentally prepared for a fail and for the supplementary exam. At least the boring subject is postponed until the re-exam date.

Mentor: That makes sense, but this relaxation is costly. Dealing with failure in the first attempt can be emotionally draining. There is no escaping the subject, you will have to study it later anyway. Supplementary exams bring extra hassle like:

- Applying on time
- Paying extra fees
- Studying this subject with your regular subjects

You might even have to study it alone. Some students intentionally skip regular exam and re-appear later. Do you think you get better marks in a supplementary exam?

Student: No, ma'am. There is always an upper limit for the highest marks you can get in a supplementary exam. So, the overall result does not improve much.

Mentor: Exactly! Ignoring a subject today brings trouble later. Have you noticed you can get many marks just by submitting assignments on time? Even doing assignments with a classmate helps you learn, and sometimes those questions come in the exam. Bonus: if you don't ignore your assignments, you need fewer marks to pass the final exam.

Student: It's true. We create trouble for ourselves when we postpone studying a subject. Thank you, ma'am, for making me aware of this. I will motivate myself every day.

Key Takeaways:

- Give your best today, not tomorrow.
- Work hard to clear your exams the first time, instead of depending on supplementary exams.
- Do your assignments on time and well – this means you will need fewer marks to pass your final exam!

Quick Adventure:

Write down the list of all subjects for which you have exams soon. Pick one you think is most difficult for you. Write one thing you can do today to prepare better for that exam.

CHAPTER SIX

APPLY AFFIRMATIONS

Shape your own mindset and never give up.

Student: Hi ma'am, I'm struggling today. For some subjects, I feel like I am not that intelligent, and I will never be able to understand them. Especially subjects that have a mathematical part, I feel scared of remembering former and doing calculations.

Mentor: It's natural to fear what you don't know. But remember: nothing is difficult once you understand it. You're stronger than you think.

Student: When I'm afraid, my energy drops and I forget this. How do I keep my mind strong?

Mentor: I have a solution for you! Train your mind with positive affirmations. What you tell yourself matters. If you say, "Physics is too hard; I'll never pass," your mind believes it and stops trying. Instead say, "Physics is tough, but I'm learning. I can master at least 60 percent." Now, your mind looks for solutions.

Student: I see, what else can I tell myself?

Mentor: Try these:

- Say "I can learn this." Remove the 't' from can't.
- Give full attention to one small part at a time.
- Use extra help: easy notes, videos, or another textbook in your own language.
- Watch solved examples, then try them yourself.
- Repeat. The more you practise, the clearer it becomes.
- Make quick notes for ideas you forget.

Repeating these quick tips or putting them on your wall can be a great reminder to keep going.

Here are some simple affirmations. Say them out loud or write them every day:

- I am smart.
- I am a fast learner.
- I can solve this problem.
- I am improving every day.

Student: Okay, I will try this. What if I lose my courage and forget to do these too? Sometimes progress is just too slow, and it's difficult to keep a positive mindset and high energy all the time.

Mentor: How do many people get rich? They treat every rupee they earn as potential for more money through investment and keep aiming higher. Keep picturing your biggest goal each day and your mind will find the way to make it real. That goal might seem far, but it is important to pat yourself when you make progress. Even if results are slow, celebrate each small step. Then moving forward with fresh energy will be easier.

Student: Thank you, ma'am! I'll start using these ideas today.

Key Takeaways:

- Repeat positive affirmations to stay motivated even when it is hard.
- Celebrate small wins and visualise big achievements.
- Keep a positive mindset and never stop trying – success comes to those who don't give up.

Quick Adventure:

Repeat 5 times: ***"I am healthy, happy, active and smart."***
Write down one of the affirmations from the list above and put it on your wallpaper or your wall.

FOCUS TECHNIQUES

In this section, we discuss various techniques improving focus and performance in studies.

CHAPTER SEVEN

Eat Your Pizza Fresh!

Waiting makes learning harder.

Mentor: Hi dear, what do you do when you go to a restaurant and order your favourite pizza?

Student: I check the menu, see the flavours and ingredients, and pick the one that suits my taste and budget.

Mentor: And when the pizza arrives, fresh and hot, what do you do?

Student: I can't wait! I slice it, add some seasoning, and take a big bite.

Mentor: Do you ever wait for it to go cold?

Student: No way! Cold pizza loses its crunch, the cheese stops melting, and it just doesn't taste the same.

Mentor: Exactly. That's how learning works. Think of your studies like eating a hot pizza. When you pick a stream — like engineering or arts — you are choosing your pizza's flavour. But once the "pizza" of a lesson is served, eat it hot. Pay attention in class, then revise the same day while it's fresh. When concepts are "hot," they're easier to understand and remember. Wait too long, and they go "cold"—harder to digest. It is a psychological fact that it is easier to remember and understand a lesson if you revise and repeat it soon after you learn it. The more you delay, the harder it gets.

Student: I see, that makes sense. I'll try to do that.

Mentor: Great! Now, do you like every pizza topping, or are there some you usually skip?

Student: I don't like mushrooms and olives, so I usually take those out of my pizza.

Mentor: That's fine! In studies, not every small topic is equally important. But never skip the "base", the main ideas that are essential. When in doubt about which topics are a 'base' and which ones are a 'topping' ask your teacher.

Student: I see, thanks! Ma'am, what if someone doesn't even like their pizza? Some students don't get to pick their subjects what should they do?

Mentor: Great question! That's a very normal scenario. Sometimes, you may have to study a subject someone else chose for you, just like trying pizza for the first time because your parents ordered it. Someone like your teachers or parents may tell you to try a subject because they know its value. You may not love it right away, but if you give it a fair chance when it's "hot", you might discover you enjoy it.

Student: That's true, Ma'am. Giving new subjects a fair chance right away makes sense. Thank you.

Key Takeaways:

- Hot pizza = Fresh concepts, easier learning; Cold pizza = Old, forgotten concepts, harder.

- Study new topics as soon as they're taught – *review on the same day*, just like eating pizza hot
- Focus on the "base" topics — don't skip them

Quick Adventure:

Tonight, pick a topic you learned today—even if it's not your favourite. Spend 10 minutes revising it or explaining it out loud. Then, write down one thing you understood well and one question you could ask your teacher. That's how you eat your pizza hot!

CHAPTER EIGHT

ONE ALPHABET AT A TIME

Take small steps to make big progress.

Mentor: Hi dear, do you remember how your teacher started teaching you the alphabet in kindergarten?

Student: Yes, Ma'am! She taught us one letter at a time. What does it look like? How is it pronounced? Which words start with that alphabet? For example, "A for Apple and Ant". She even showed us pictures. It was such a nice time when I used to repeat one alphabet at a time and learn different things about it.

Mentor: If your teacher had made you learn A to Z in one go, would you have remembered anything?

Student: No, Ma'am. I would have been confused and probably forgotten most of it.

Mentor: That's right. When you try to study everything at once—maybe right before exams—it feels like climbing a giant mountain. Sometimes, the chapter you need is buried at the bottom of that stack. Digging out that chapter, you feel tired, stressed, and nothing sticks in your mind.

Instead, you can break your work into small, manageable chunks. Just like learning one alphabet per day, focus on a little at a time. When you do something small every day, it feels easy—and soon, you have learned a lot without even realising it.

Student: But, ma'am, the syllabus is so vast now!

Mentor: You are right! But even now, your teacher gives you one part of the syllabus at a time. Consistency is the key to success. Try to study every subject every day. If that's not practical, focus on two or three subjects each day. This helps in two ways:

- You have less to do in one day, so it feels easier.
- When you learn a little at a time, it's easier to remember and repeat what you've learned.

Student: That makes sense. I'll try to do that.

Mentor: Great, now imagine you learned the letter "C" one day, but never practiced it again. You would forget how to write "C" or which words start with it. The same thing happens with studies. If you read something once and never look at it again, it disappears from your memory.

Student: Yeah, sometimes I think I know a subject but can't recall it properly during exams.

Mentor: That's because we underestimate the power of repetition. Even easy subjects need revising. Confidence comes from repeating the small and easy things. Go back and practice what you learned—just like tracing each letter many times in your notebook. A little repetition every day makes your memory strong and your learning easy.

Student: You're right. I feel motivated. I'll go study for many hours today!

Mentor: Wait! If your teacher made you practice the whole alphabet for six hours straight, how would you feel?

Student: Tired and bored. My brain would stop working.

Mentor: That's what happens when you study for hours without a break. Try the Pomodoro technique:

1. Study one small thing for 25 minutes (like learning one letter).
2. Take a 5-minute break—walk around, drink water, or just relax.
3. Then, start the next 25-minute session.

After a few sessions, your brain will stay fresh.

Student: Ah I see, so dragging study time with unbroken focus for hours isn't as good as I thought it was. Thank you, Ma'am. I will try this out

Key Takeaways:

- Break your work into small, manageable parts. Study in small portions regularly, not all at exam time
- Use the Pomodoro Technique to keep study sessions short and focused
- Repeat each small topic to build it in your memory.

Quick Adventure:

Today, pick one very short topic. Set a timer for 25 minutes. Study only that topic, then take a 5-minute break.

CHAPTER NINE

SERIES VERSUS MOVIES

Embrace your inner filmy and stay in sequence.

Mentor: Hi dear, when you go to a movie in a theatre, what do you do?

Student: I reach early. I settle in my seat and make sure I can see the screen clearly. Sometimes, I reach even before time so I that I can get snacks from the cinema canteen. I make sure nothing will disturb me during the movie.

Mentor: So you like to settle down and relax before the first scene starts. And when the movie begins?

Student: I focus 100% on the screen, dialogues and the story. I don't want to miss anything. I paid for the ticket after all!

Mentor: Exactly! Think of your class like a movie, 40 minutes or an hour long. The better you listen, more you will understand the "story" and enjoy. Here are some tips to help you focus and get the most out of every class. Make it a blockbuster!

- Arrive early and choose a good seat before the teacher enters. Make sure you can see and hear clearly.
- Settle down before the lesson starts. Keep your books, pen, and notes ready.
- Take notes during class. Write down important points, just like you'd remember the best lines in a movie.
- Stay attentive the whole time. If you stay focused, you'll remember the lesson, just like you remember a good film.

Student: Ah, makes sense. Treating a lecture like a movie. But sometimes, it all goes over my head.

Mentor: Some topics in some subjects are like movies—complete in one or two classes, easy to understand. Other topics are like a web series—you need to learn them in sequence. Tell me, how do you usually watch a series?

Student: For a series, you need to watch it in order. You can't skip episodes.

Mentor: Exactly! Now suppose you and your friend start watching start with Episode 1. Later he watches Episode 2 without you, and next time he's on Episode 3. Would you jump straight to Episode 3 with him?

Student: No, Ma'am! I wouldn't spoil the sequence. I would first catch Episode 2 and then continue with episode 3, even if I had to watch it alone.

Mentor: Perfect. The same logic applies to your classes. YDon't jump ahead if you miss something. Cover the "episode" you skipped, then join the current one. Make sure that before you go to a class, you have tried your best to cover up all the 'episodes' for that topic before this one!

Student: Yes, Ma'am! I'll keep these points in mind. Hopefully, the story of the lecture will make sense.

Key Takeaways:

- Treat lecture like a movie theatre hall, arrive early, choose a good seat and pay attention.
- For "movie" topics: learn them quickly and finish completely.
- For "series" topics: study in order and make good notes, so you don't lose the story.

Quick Adventure:

Take 5 minutes right now to organize your study spot at home—put your books, notes, and pen in place, so you're ready for your next "movie" (class) with no distractions.

CHAPTER TEN

PROGRESS TRACKER

Track where your time goes.

Student: Ma'am, do you have a simple way to help me keep track of what I need to study, and how much time I should give to each subject?

Mentor: Sure! First, tell me—how do you plan your day right now?

Student: Honestly, I do make a schedule and write down all my tasks. But I mostly end up doing what I enjoy more. Like, I never miss my table tennis time, even if I'm tired or busy. Sometimes, I even skip class to play!

Mentor: That's very honest. It seems like you have many things to do. But there is only so much time in one day. Most of us end up doing our favourite things first and sometimes skip the harder or less fun things. Often, studies are the first thing to drop. That's why a progress tracker can help.

Try this: Write down all the activities you want to do each day—study, games, anything important. At the end of the day, put a tick next to the things you did, and put a cross out next to what you missed. Please refer to the end of chapter to see an example of a progress tracker. Do this for a few days.

This can be a useful way to find out which direction you are going in, and accordingly be more intentional about which direction you want to go in. You'll see what you're skipping, and what you're spending the most time on. You might notice you need to add more time for studying or cut down a little on other things. That way, you can choose better tomorrow.

A progress tracker is flexible—you can add new activities or remove old ones whenever you want.

Student: That makes sense, Ma'am. I'll start using a tracker to see where my time really goes.

Key Takeaways:

- Arrange all your daily tasks by priority
- Check your tracker every few days to see your progress and adjust

Quick Adventure:

Make a simple tracker for today. List all your planned activities. At night, put a tick or a cross next to each one. Do this for one week and see where your time goes!

Progress Tracker Example

Progress Tracker Example							
Month:	Week:						
	Mon	Tues	Wed	Thurs	Fri	Sat	Sun
Studying	√ 6		√ 1		√ 3		√ 4
Playing Guitar	√ 2	√ 0.5		√ 2			
Swimming	√ 2						
Social media		√ 2		√ 1		√ 2	√ 2
Activity 5			√ 5				
Activity 6		√ 4					
Activity 7	√ 1				√ 3		

Optional: You can add the number of hours spent on each activity next to it.

Progress Tracker Example

CHAPTER ELEVEN

PARETO PRINCIPLE (80/20 RULE)

Work smart, not hard.

Mentor: Hi dear, do you know about the Pareto Principle, also called the 80/20 rule? It says that 20% of causes lead to 80% of outcomes. In other words, a small number of things have a big impact.

Student: That's interesting. So, you can focus on the most important 20% to solve most of the problem. Does this idea apply to studying?

Mentor: Yes, it does. Think about when you start a new subject and find it difficult. What usually happens?

Student: Sometimes, if I don't understand the first few classes, and then miss a couple more, the whole subject becomes too hard. After that, I just stop reading it.

Mentor: This is common, but you don't have to see the whole subject as difficult. Usually, there are some parts that are easier and some that are harder. The smart way is to find which parts are easy for you and start with those. If you're not sure, ask a teacher or a senior to help you identify the "must-do" parts. Try to cover the part that you can manage first.

Student: So, should I leave the harder parts for later?

Mentor: Yes—if your exam doesn't require you to answer every section, focus first on the parts that will get you the most marks. Once you've done those, go back and try the tougher sections if you have time. Just make sure you don't skip the basics or any compulsory topics.

Student: That really changes how I look at difficult subjects!

Mentor: Exactly. Work smarter, not just harder. Cover the easy parts well and revise them. Build your confidence. Then, try the difficult parts—maybe with friends or with help—after you have a good foundation. Even if you can't master everything, you'll still be able to answer many questions on the exam!

Student: Thank you, Ma'am! This is a great way to cover the syllabus.

Key Takeaways:

- Focus first on the 70–80% of a subject that feels manageable
- Study the more difficult 20–30% in a group or with help

Quick Adventure:

List all the chapters or topics for that subject. Circle the ones you think are easier and most important. Today, spend 20 minutes reviewing just one important topic.

CHAPTER TWELVE

OLD QUESTION PAPERS

Recognise patterns and learn to solve.

Mentor: Hi dear, tell me how you feel when you face exam questions and appear for an exam for the first time?

Student: Honestly, Ma'am, I feel a lot of fear! I feel a bit more relaxed if teachers give us an idea of the exam pattern or share a sample paper. But when we don't know what kind of questions will come, it's always a challenge to attempt the paper.

Mentor: I understand. Here's the good part: most exam questions are based on what's already been taught in class, and the content doesn't change much from year to year. So, this time, questions will be based on the same content as before.

Also, many students have taken these exams in the past, and their old question papers are available. Using old papers, or speaking to seniors, is one of the best ways to prepare and score well.

Student: That's a good idea, Ma'am! What are the benefits of using old question papers?

Mentor: Here's how it helps: Start by collecting old question papers. If you can get the solutions as well, even better—half your work is done and you can jump right into revising. If not, try to match the questions from the papers with your syllabus and find the answers in your textbook, on the internet, or by asking your teachers.

Once you have the solutions, there are many benefits:

1. You'll know what type of questions have been asked and the kind of answers expected.
2. If any questions are repeated (which happens often), you'll be ready. This will boost your confidence and help you answer quickly and correctly.
3. It saves you time and energy during the actual exam. You'll be familiar with the format, and answering repeated questions quickly will give you more time for new questions.

Student: Thank you, Ma'am! I will surely try this.

Key Takeaways:

- Collect old question papers for your subjects—from teachers, seniors, or other resources
- Practice solutions from old papers to understand the patterns

Quick Adventure:

Download previous year question papers for one of your subjects.

BEYOND THE CLASSROOM

In this section, we discuss how you can balance studies with things outside your classroom – like heath, relationships and hobbies.

CHAPTER THIRTEEN

HEALTHY IS WEALTHY

Build good habits for the body and the mind.

Mentor: Hi dear, tell me how much you take care of your health?

Student: A lot! I do my fitness routine daily. I enjoy it. But sometimes during exam season, I miss it and need to see a psychologist or counsellor to help me handle the stress of exams and results.

Mentor: Yes, that's a concern for all of us. These days, we emphasize both students' physical and mental health equally. When students have stress or anxiety, they cannot focus on their studies and may need to consult a psychologist. The doctor might find they don't feel like studying, but often the problem isn't just mental—it's physical as well. First, you should be physically well. This is your first duty to your body, because "a healthy mind resides in a healthy body." If you keep falling sick, it will affect your attendance and make it harder to keep up in class. Many problems start with health issues.

Student: Yes Ma'am! When we have even a small headache, we don't feel like listening to the teacher. Sometimes we get irritated at people around us, nothing tastes good, and we can't do anything at all. So, it's very important to keep ourselves healthy; that is our first duty.

Mentor: It's truly said: health is wealth. Your performance is important, but even more important is not having any illness. Love nature, get up early, and have a good health routine. You will have better physical and mental health when you have enough energy in your body and mind.

Student: Yes Ma'am, it's true. Even our parents worry when we fall sick. We need to take care of ourselves, especially when we are away from home. It's even more difficult when we miss assignments or evaluations. That's why many students now have a routine for playing sports.

Mentor: Yes, that's a very good habit. But not everyone exercises regularly. You don't have to be on the sports ground every day to be fit. A daily routine of 15 to 30 minutes of simple exercise, yoga, pranayama or meditation in your room or a common place can be just as effective. Think of it like brushing your teeth, but for your whole body. It's also perfect "me time."

Here's the catch: you can only do this if you get up on time in the morning—and that's only possible if you sleep on time. Good sleep is very important for health. It's the main source of energy for our body, just like electricity charges a mobile phone or laptop.

Another main source of energy is healthy food. Good, healthy food is served at home or in the hostel mess, but students often skip regular meals and order junk food. Tell me, do you prefer junk food regularly or only at parties?

Student: Ma'am, I am careful about this. If I keep ordering junk food, it affects my health and also increases expenses. So, I prefer to have things like pizza, burgers, and cold drinks only at parties. Thank you for the useful advice about good health. I will try to be a healthy person.

Key Takeaways:

- Health affects everything else – prioritise it!
- Maintain a routine with exercise and good sleep
- Avoid junk food

Quick Adventure:

Close your eyes and take 5 deep breaths. Next, go for a walk or a run today. Or, do any exercise for 15 minutes.

CHAPTER FOURTEEN

ENTERTAINMENT AS A REWARD

Save the best for later, it'll be more delicious.

Mentor: Hi dear, how important do you think entertainment is for students?

Student: A lot. Entertainment is one way of relaxing and re-energizing oneself.

Mentor: Absolutely true. Everyone has the right to entertainment. When we relax—like watching a movie on TV or in a theatre—we enjoy ourselves. But think about it: when we enjoy a film, we pay for that with our money, time, and attention. That's why we should treat entertainment with care. It should be a reward, not a distraction. If you scroll through social media or watch a film before finishing your work, you're using time that could help you reach your goals.

Student: Yes, Ma'am. I've felt that. Sometimes, I sit down with friends to watch something "just for a bit"—and before I know it, hours have passed. Afterwards, I'm too tired to study or focus on anything.

Mentor: This is the drawback of choosing entertainment over work. You're choosing easy joy over meaningful progress. Greater happiness comes when you achieve your goals and then celebrate with some entertainment.

Student: I see! That makes sense. But what about hobbies? I barely get time for them in my packed schedule with classes, assignments, and job preparation. Should I be making more time for them?

Mentor: It's true, your schedule as a student is packed. Let me ask you: Are you really attending your classes with full attention? It's worth considering:

- Are you really following the schedule for classes?
- Can you say you're attending classes with 100% focus?
- Are your assignments being done sincerely, or just copied in a hurry to meet deadlines?

It's worth pausing for a second to think about how much time goes into complaining about deadlines. Often, we confuse being busy with being productive. We say there's no time for hobbies, but we don't stop to examine where our time is really going.

If you give 90–100% focus to your classes today, you'll spend less time relearning or preparing for job interviews later. Then, you'll discover pockets of time and energy that can be spent on things you love.

Student: That's true Ma'am. I agree with you. But where do hobbies fit in here?

Mentor: Hobbies come from the soul. If you love singing, you don't need motivation or energy to sing, even after a tiring day. Hobbies don't drain energy; they boost your energy and help you come up with new ideas. So, when you have many things in your schedule, why not keep some time for a hobby as well?

Even small acts—like maintaining a blog, drawing, recording music, attending workshops, or participating in college festivals—can give you a sense of achievement and a new perspective. Sharing these joys, whether in person or online, can help build your self-esteem and self-respect.

One of my old students was a very good writer. Spending some time on writing each week contributed to her success story. Her teachers and classmates respected her in a new way, and even though she wasn't a topper in her studies, she felt a sense of achievement when her writing was appreciated.

Student: You are right, Ma'am! Many times, we get extra credits for extra-curricular activities and achievements.

Mentor: Yes, extra-curricular activities add value to your resume as well. When your soul is happy with your achievements, you can shift your focus to studies too.

Student: Yes, Ma'am, I now realise continuing our hobbies on a regular basis is important. It doesn't waste time—it adds energy and a sense of accomplishment.

Key Takeaways:

- Don't entertain first and drain all your energy
- Don't confuse being busy with being productive
- Work first with full focus, entertain afterwards to celebrate success
- Spend some time on your hobbies and pat yourself for your achievements in extra-curricular activities.

Quick Adventure:

Make a list of things you will allow yourself to do only after studying.

49

Quick Adventure:

Make a list of things you will allow yourself to do only after studying.

CHAPTER FIFTEEN

STAY CONNECTED

Find and make the most of the people in your life.

Mentor: Hi dear, tell how you feel when you hear or read about someone's success story?

Student: I just think, "Wow! What a success! What great work!" and then I clap.

Mentor: See how easy it is to clap for others. The best example is film award shows for entertainment—we spend so much time watching who gets nominated and who wins. But it shouldn't stop there. The important thing is to learn from their journey. What is their success mantra? How did they reach that level?
Now, speaking to famous actors might be difficult, but this also applies to your seniors or classmates in college who win medals or prizes. Try to learn from them, too.

Student: Ma'am, how can we learn from them? I usually don't contact them much, especially after they graduate.

Mentor: You should! Be friendly and try to get good tips. It won't harm them, and it can benefit you a lot. Based on their experience, your classmates or seniors may share methods that suit your style. Follow their tips, try them out in your routine, and see if they help. At the end of the day, don't just clap for others—work hard so that you can applaud yourself, too.

Student: Thank you, Ma'am!

Mentor: Great! Also, connect with your family members regularly and update them about your progress. This will bring happiness to you and to them. If any family member has knowledge about your subject, discussing it with them can really help. Do you have a mentor at your school or college?

Student: Yes, Ma'am! I have a mentor who I meet to discuss any issues I'm facing. She motivates me whenever we meet. But my friend doesn't bother meeting with his mentor.

Mentor: Having a mentor in school or college is a great support for students. Attending meetings with your mentor and following their advice is an easy way to solve many problems. Tell your friend about the positive vibes you get from meeting your mentor—maybe he will be motivated to attend, too. A mentor can only help if students cooperate.

Key Takeaways:

- Asking for help from mentors, peers and parents is great in the long run – don't hesitate to reach out!
- Staying connected brings happiness

Quick Adventure:

Call a family member and share one achievement from today.

The Power of Helping

Build confidence by serving others.

Mentor: Hi dear, we talked about getting help—never be afraid to ask for it. At the same time, helping others is a great habit. Do you take part in any social service?

Student: Never, Ma'am! My schedule is fully packed. I'm not even sure what kind of social service I can do.

Mentor: Social service can sound big and time-consuming, but it doesn't always mean large projects. You can help in small ways, like teaching phone apps to students or staff who need it, or helping someone learn a new language or skill, like art. Even just 1–2 hours a week—or even a month—is a first step to contributing to society and being a good human being. These small acts may seem tiny, but they can make a big difference for someone else and add to your own self-worth.

Helping your juniors with subjects you know well is also social service. One of my mentees started a "Support Squad" in her final year. She would meet juniors once a week to solve their doubts in different areas, such as:

- Preparing for interviews
- Revising important subjects
- Providing old question papers with solutions
- Connecting them to extra-curricular clubs
- Raising funds for needy workers in college

This social service helped her improve herself, and she earned a lot of respect from club members and teachers. She even got great recommendations, which were very helpful later.

Student: Yes, Ma'am! I can teach new students or staff how to use some phone apps. I'll try to start during my entertainment time. Just thinking about it is making me happy.

Key Takeaways:

- Helping others also helps you grow.
- Start small: every act of help counts.

Quick Adventure:

Do one act of kindness today. It can even be as simple as taking a round and switching-off all lights and fans not in use.